Celebrating

VICTORIA

M000251887

VICTORIA · VANCOUVER · CALGARY

Copyright © 2000, 2010 John Walls
Heritage House edition 2010

All rights reserved. No part of this publication may be reproduced, stored in a retrieval system
or transmitted in any form or by any means—electronic, mechanical, audio recording or
otherwise—without the written permission of the publisher or a photocopying licence from
Access Copyright, Toronto, Canada.

Heritage House Publishing Company Ltd.
heritagehouse.ca

LIBRARY AND ARCHIVES CANADA CATALOGUING IN PUBLICATION

Walls, John, 1953–
Celebrating Victoria / John Walls.
ISBN 978-1-926613-76-5
1. Victoria (B.C.)—Pictorial works. I. Title.
FC3846.37.W36 2010   971.1'28050222   C2010-901824-9

All photographs by John Walls except pages 5 inset (Royal BC Museum, BC Archives, B-09502),
15 (Royal BC Museum, BC Archives, A-01253), 18 top (Dennis Schmidt), 27 inset (The Butchart
Gardens), 31 top (The Butchart Gardens), back cover (The Butchart Gardens).

front cover The British Columbia Parliament Buildings at dusk provide
an illuminated backdrop to Victoria's picturesque Inner Harbour.
back cover The Sunken Garden at The Butchart Gardens.

This book was produced using FSC-certified, acid-free paper,
processed chlorine free and printed with vegetable-based inks.

We acknowledge the financial support of the Government of Canada
through the Canada Book Fund and the Canada Council for the Arts, and the
province of British Columbia through the British Columbia Arts Council
and the Book Publishing Tax Credit.

Printed in Canada

19 18 17 16 3 4 5 6

Welcome to Victoria, Canada's most beautiful city. From flowers to whales, from totem poles to fine tea, Victoria appeals to a wide array of tastes and interests.

Dating back to 1592 when Juan de Fuca explored the west coast, Victoria has enjoyed an exciting history. Today it is best known as a "British-style" city, with the kind of shops, antique dealers and beautiful gardens typically found in England.

top A bagpiper welcomes visitors to Victoria's Inner Harbour, in front of the Fairmont Empress Hotel and the Parliament Buildings.

middle BC Ferries provides frequent daily service to Vancouver Island.

bottom The *Coho* plies the waters between the state of Washington and Vancouver Island.

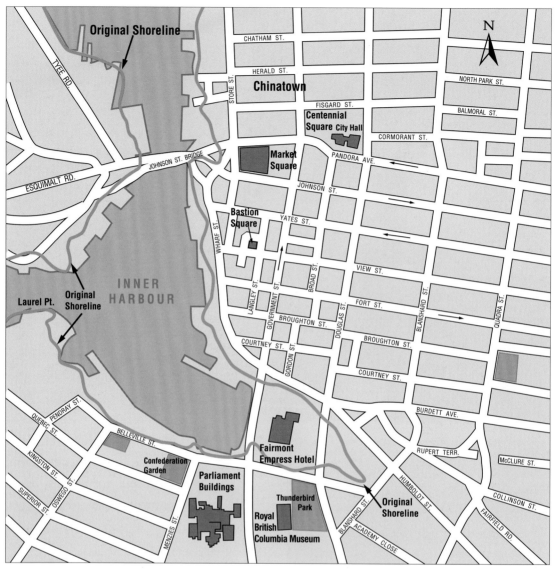

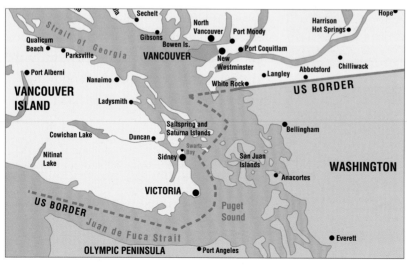

Street map of the Inner Harbour area of Victoria. Victoria is the capital city of the province of British Columbia. It is located on the southern tip of Vancouver Island on Canada's Pacific coast.

Finished in 1908, the Canadian Pacific's Empress Hotel (now the Fairmont Empress) quickly became an attraction on its own. The main centre block was designed by Francis Rattenbury *(inset)*, who also designed the Parliament Buildings, the Canadian Pacific Marine Terminal and many outstanding private residences in Victoria.

Rattenbury was one of Victoria's most celebrated citizens, until a nasty scandal over an affair with a younger woman drove him to live in England. He eventually met an untimely and brutal end at the hands of his houseboy, who, so the story goes, was himself involved with Rattenbury's new young bride.

The Empress was expanded in 1910, 1913 and 1929, and extensively renovated in 1989. Today the Fairmont Empress is home to the world-famous Tea Lobby where a traditional Afternoon Tea is served (call the hotel for reservations and for tour information).

above This view shows the Fairmont Empress Hotel from across the Inner Harbour.

following pages The magnificent Fairmont Empress stands at the foot of the Inner Harbour, the focus of Victoria's downtown area.

The Inner Harbour is the heart and soul of Victoria. It was chosen as the site for a major port by the Hudson's Bay Company in 1843, and within a few years came to play a large role in the region's economic development. In fact, up until the 20th century, Victoria was the largest port north of San Francisco.

above This photo of a First Nations dugout canoe and the *Victoria Clipper* is a study in contrasts between two eras and two cultures.

opposite top Victoria's Inner Harbour is a popular destination for residents, visitors and tourists alike. You can expect to encounter buskers, jugglers, performers on stilts and a variety of vendors eager to sell their wares or sketch your portrait.

opposite bottom It also serves as a seaport and seaplane airport. Stay long enough and you'll get a chance to see one glide down gracefully from the sky and taxi along the waterway.

With the increasing importance of the railways, this status was soon transferred to the mainland ports of Seattle and Vancouver.

After 1900, Victoria became more important as a tourist destination than as a maritime port. Consequently, the Inner Harbour is surrounded by hotels, shops and residential areas, with the harbour catering to small craft, larger ferries and sea planes. Many of Victoria's major attractions ring the harbour: the Royal British Columbia Museum, Thunderbird Park, the Fairmont Empress, the Pacific Undersea Gardens, the provincial Parliament Buildings and many sightseeing and whale-watching operations.

Victoria's waterfront is a focused miscellany of sights, sounds and atmospheres. At dusk throughout the year, the Parliament Buildings are outlined in white lights, casting a festive and joyful reflection on the water of the Inner Harbour.

Victoria's waterfront is also an excellent place to stroll on a warm summer evening. The sound of the water lapping at the docks and the call of the seagulls as they fly overhead provide a wonderful counterpoint to the normal street sounds of city activity.

During the summer months, concerts are given at the Inner Harbour. One of the most popular of these is the "Symphony Splash" performed annually each August.

British Columbia's elected provincial politicians meet in the legislative chamber of Victoria's Parliament Buildings. Victoria has been a seat of government since 1859 when the region was ruled by a colonial government. Today it is the provincial capital.

The Parliament Buildings were designed by Francis Rattenbury in 1893 and completed in 1898. Subsequent additions were made in 1912 and 1915.

The interior of the Parliament Buildings is handsomely decorated with frescoes extolling the rich resources of the region, marble cladding and stunning stained glass windows.

The central dome is capped with a statue of George Vancouver, who explored the coastal waters around Vancouver Island and the mainland between 1792 and 1794, claiming this area for the British Empire.

On the grounds of the Parliament Buildings is a statue of Queen Victoria, for whom the city was named. She reigned at a time when the British Empire had reached its greatest strength. Nearby is a redwood tree that is over 150 years old.

above The Parliament Buildings provide a classic backdrop to the busy Inner Harbour, whose oceanside walkway and marina are very popular during the summer tourist season.

opposite The white lights that outline the Parliament Buildings from dusk to dawn were first installed in 1897 to commemorate Queen Victoria's Diamond Jubilee. They have been a continuing Victoria tradition since then.

Craigdarroch Castle *(top)* was the luxurious project of Robert Dunsmuir *(right)*, who built the castle in 1887 in order to symbolize his successful climb to the pinnacle of wealth and power in British Columbia. Dunsmuir died in 1889, before the castle was finished. His death brought strife to the family. Contrary to verbal promises made to his sons, he left his entire estate and business holdings to his wife, Joan. This was a blow to both James and Alex (then in their 30s), who had worked in the family business all their lives. Joan lived in the castle until she died in 1908.

The castle features magnificent woodwork imported from Chicago, stained glass, and parquet floors. Craigdarroch Castle is a must-see for any visitor to Victoria.

opposite top The popular Tally-Ho takes sightseers around the town for a leisurely spin.

opposite bottom Adjoining the Fairmont Empress Hotel is the Victoria Conference Centre, a bright, modern building that provides space for meetings of all sizes.

owntown Victoria combines culture, museums, shopping, sightseeing and a variety of restaurants and hotels within one easily walked area. This makes Victoria a very foot-friendly city, inviting all to stroll along the quaint streets and busy harbour.

above The Royal BC Museum is home to natural history displays, dioramas of local ecosystems, a modern history gallery and extensive First Nations exhibits.

right A Royal BC Museum showcase display features artifacts from its collection.

opposite top The arch at the foot of Fisgard Street marks the entrance to Victoria's Chinatown.

opposite bottom Victoria's Chinatown, located right in the heart of downtown, is the oldest in Canada and the second oldest in North America, after San Francisco. Its history reaches back to the mid-nineteenth century.

opposite top Orca whales can be identified by the shape and markings of their dorsal fins. The mist is created by the whale's breath.

opposite bottom A harbour seal glides through the water. They are common sights along the Victoria coast.

above top Victoria is an extremely popular cruise ship destination for tourists worldwide and hosts over 200 vessels a year.

above An orca off the coast of Victoria.

bottom right The Fisgard Lighthouse, accessible by footpath, is the oldest lighthouse on Canada's Pacific coast.

Thunderbird Park contains the largest open-air display of totem poles anywhere. Most are replicas of poles stored in the museum and were carved in workshops on site. The current workshop is a replica of a traditional Haida house. The poles represent a number of tribal traditions: Haida, Tsimshian, Nuxalk (Bella Coola) and Kwakwaka'wakw. The park's crowning glory is Wa'waditla House, created by the world-famous carver Mungo Martin, Chief NaKap'anKam. It is an important site for First Nations ceremonies.

above The Fairmont Empress Hotel framed by totem poles.

bottom Totem pole detail.

opposite The newest pole, erected in 1999, features a thunderbird and a whale and was carved by Kwakwaka'wakw artists Johnathan Henderson and Sean Whonnock.

Beacon Hill Park *(above)*, just a five-minute walk from downtown, is one of Victoria's best-loved parks. It contains all manner of attractions: a formal garden, beds of flowers dotted throughout the park, a children's petting zoo, playgrounds, stone bridges, a

children's water park, cricket fields, pitch-and-putt golf, spectacular seaside cliffs and footpaths, running trails and benches.

The park takes its name from the torch that burned atop the hill in the 1850s to guide ships near the entrance to Victoria Harbour. In 1889, John Blair, a Scottish landscape architect, began the development of the land as a park.

opposite bottom Pom Pom dahlias blooming in Beacon Hill Park.

The Butchart Gardens

One of the most popular attractions in the Victoria area is The Butchart Gardens. Located just a few miles from Victoria's busy downtown area, the tranquil gardens are a must-see for all visitors.

Pictured here is the famous Rose Garden.

Mrs. Jennie Butchart *(right)* is generally regarded as the impetus behind the creation of The Butchart Gardens. With the help of Isaburo Kishida, she placed a Japanese garden to the north of her home in 1906. In 1909 she began planting flowers in her husband's abandoned limestone quarry. Aided by workers from his cement factory, she had tons of rich topsoil transported to the empty pit. Gradually the barren quarry underwent a magical transformation.

The creation of the Sunken Garden was Mrs. Butchart's own special project; it became the centrepiece of the varied gardens in her floral estate. A former tennis court became the Italian Garden; a vegetable patch the famous Rose Garden.

So popular were the new gardens that by 1915 tea was being served to some 18,000 people annually.

opposite The Italian Garden with its central fountain and lily pond.

above Flowers are the specialty of The Butchart Gardens, which now attracts more than a million visitors annually.

The Sunken Garden (pictured here) is The Butchart Gardens' signature garden, with flowering shrubs and bed after bed of colourful perennials and annuals. A stream flows under the walkway, a waterfall cascades from the cliffs of the old quarry, and, at the far end of the Sunken Garden, the magnificent Ross Fountain sends its dance of water skyward in an ever-changing display.

top At night, myriad hidden lights transform The Butchart Gardens into a fantasy world.

opposite Winding pathways and bridges lead to quiet corners in the Japanese Garden.

above left and right Art and nature, in the form of lights and flowers, can eerily resemble each other, as these photographs show. Fireworks are a special attraction on Saturday evenings in July and August.

The Butchart Gardens is more than a horticultural wonder. It has evolved into a wide-ranging attraction that features fine restaurants, a large, diverse gift shop, musical entertainment and seasonal displays. The Christmastime display, in particular, shows The Butchart Gardens bedecked in an enchanting array of lights.

During summer evenings, thousands of hidden lights illuminate the Gardens (*opposite*) and sculptures, such as *The Three Sturgeons* (*left*), which came from Italy in 1975. The Ross Fountain in the Sunken Garden also features special evening lighting. The fountain, as well as the beautiful lighting illuminations, were installed by Ian Ross, son of Jennie Butchart's eldest daughter.

Ashort distance outside of downtown Victoria lies another world: the rural charm and spectacular natural beauty of Vancouver Island. From rugged cliffs to gentle beaches, from deep, dark forests to open farmlands with grazing sheep, Vancouver Island is a diverse region that provides the curious visitor with countless days of exploration.

When James Douglas landed in this area in 1843 he proclaimed it to be "a perfect Eden." And so it remains to this day. Vancouver Island's inherent qualities of beauty, peace and natural magnificence have enticed many travellers to return — or perhaps even to move — to this little slice of heaven right here on earth.

top A waterfall splashes over the golden rock of Mystic Beach along the Juan de Fuca Marine Trail.

bottom Sunsets provide us with a time to capture a peaceful moment at the end of a day.